D1714990

The Essential D. G. Jones

The Essential
D. G. Jones

selected by Jim Johnstone

The Porcupine's Quill

Library and Archives Canada Cataloguing in Publication

Jones, D.G. (Douglas Gordon), 1929–
[Poems. Selections]
   The essential D.G. Jones / selected by Jim Johnstone.

(Essential poets series ; 14)
Includes bibliographical references.
ISBN 978-0-88984-398-1 (paperback)

   I. Johnstone, Jim, 1978 –, editor   II. Title.   III. Title: Poems.
Selections.   IV. Series: Essential poets series ; 14

PS8519.O53A6 2016   C811'.54   C2016-904289-8

Published by The Porcupine's Quill, 68 Main Street, PO Box 160,
Erin, Ontario NOB 1T0. http://porcupinesquill.ca

Edited by Jim Johnstone.
Represented in Canada by Canadian Manda.
Trade orders are available from University of Toronto Press.

We acknowledge the support of the Ontario Arts Council and the Canada
Council for the Arts for our publishing program. The financial support of
the Government of Canada through the Canada Book Fund is also
gratefully acknowledged.

Table of Contents

Foreword

The poetry of D.G. Jones demands a change of pace from readers submerged in the digital age. Full of subtle shifts in diction, tone and voice, his work is elemental and, like the sun and snow he so often conjures, offers a portal to the natural world. Consider a poem like 'Portrait of Anne Hébert', which begins with sunlight brightening a table before a 'draught at the window' announces the French-Canadian poet's presence. The room opens with surgical precision; and read slowly, the matter-of-fact voice warms with small details, imbuing Hébert with a grace that complements her air of authority. In Jones's hands, the poem approaches self-portraiture, particularly when Hébert's words 'make an incision / Probing / The obscure disease', pairing the two authors by virtue of their technical prowess. There's an intricacy in the Rorschach blot–like 'tatter of lace' that covers the page, one where speed is counter to comprehension, and the world pauses to reveal its peculiarities.

'Portrait of Anne Hébert' is firmly rooted in the modernist tradition, and is an appropriate opening to a book that traces not just the evolution of a poet, but the radical break with poetic tradition that marks the end of the 20th century. D.G. Jones's poetry straddles — and in many ways epitomizes the increasing fragmentation that defines — the postmodern age. His first book, *Frost on the Sun* (1957), published by Contact Press after he finished his M.A. in English Literature at Queen's University, is also his most formal. Released the same year as Ted Hughes's *The Hawk in the Rain*, the best poems in the book, like 'Northern Water Thrush' and 'Winterkill', share Hughes's metaphysical preoccupations. These poems were reprinted in Jones's next collection, *The Sun is Axeman* (1961), which is essentially a second take on his debut, even down to the detail of the sun in the title. *The Essential D.G. Jones* begins here, as it exhibits the first iteration of the author's mature style.

Formally, Jones's first three books could be considered a trilogy. Rigorous, controlled, and for the most part written in regular meter, the poems Jones composed in the 1960s often subvert what Northrop Frye described as Canada's 'garrison mentality'.[1] In his book of criticism, *Butterfly on Rock* (1970), Jones argues for Canadian writers who 'knock down the walls and let the wilderness in', communicating with their environment rather than letting it define them. His own work reflects this approach; by the time he released *Phrases from Orpheus* in 1967, Jones wrote like a poet at home in the national landscape. Consider this excerpt from 'The Perishing Bird', one of Canada's most enduring lyrics:

> For the mind in time
> Is a perishing bird,
> It sings and is still.
>
> It comes and goes like the butterflies
> Who visit the hill.
>
> The cries of the children come on the wind
> And are gone. The wild bees come,
> And the clouds.
>
> And the mind is not
> A place at all,
> But a harmony of now,
>
> The necessary angel, slapping
> Flies in its own sweat.

By likening human thought to an ecosystem that contains birds, bees and butterflies, Jones tears down the wall between man and the outside world. His vision is specific, and he clarifies that 'the mind is not / A place at all', but the comings and goings of the world's creatures, which he dubs 'a harmony of now'. In an omnibus review of Jones's work entitled 'Coming Home to the World', George Bowering singles out 'The Perishing Bird' as a refutation of W.B. Yeats's 'Sailing to Byzantium'.[2] The comparison is apt, as the holy city that Yeats imagines shuts out 'Fish, flesh, [and] fowl', and is erected to keep 'any natural thing' at bay.

The early 1970s marked the first significant shift in D.G. Jones's poetics. His newly integrated vision of the Canadian landscape began to include the page itself, with space modifying both his voice and his rhetoric. This culminated in the Governor General's Award–winning collection *Under the Thunder the Flowers Light Up the Earth* (1977), a book notable for its lean, knife-like stanzas. Gone were the capital letters at the beginning of each line, and instead a looser, more instinctual technique pervades poems like 'A Garland of Milne' and 'Winter Comes Hardly'. The first two lines of the former, 'He lived in the bush, the wilderness / but he made light of it', typifies the poet's wit, which complements the poem's associative diction. Wry, and often biting, particularly as Jones relaxed into a poetics more his own, these comic moments give the work from this period a distinct sense of levity.

While he was positioned at the Université de Sherbrooke (1963–1994), Jones's Canada became less a country of 'two solitudes' (a term popularized by the Hugh MacLennan novel of the same name), and more a place where 'translation [was] in the wind'.[3] As the co-founder of the bilingual literary journal *ellipse*, Jones played an active role in the promotion of Québécois literature, sponsoring reciprocal translation among Canadian authors. He also began publishing book-length translations of several Québécois poets, including Paul-Marie Lapointe (1976, 1985), Gaston Miron (1984) and Normand de Bellefeuille (1992). Conscious of the national movement to preserve French as one of Canada's official tongues — particularly the multicultural initiatives of the Trudeau government — Jones's verse became startlingly fluent, generating what he referred to as 'a more intimate commerce between the two languages'.[4] This is exemplified by poems like 'I Annihilate', which swings between French and English without warning, and 'A Thousand Hooded Eyes' where Jones scatters dialectical notes as if he were composing jazz.

Linguistic flexibility continued to be one of the hallmarks of Jones's ever-evolving body of work throughout the 1980s and 1990s, and books like *The Floating Garden* (1995) and *Wild Asterisks in Cloud* (1997) underscore the author's experimental instincts, which evolved well into the postmodern age. Sun and snow are still Jones's primary archetypes, but his late poems display a heightened existential awareness, blending the interior and exterior worlds of their protagonists. Take 'Praise', reprinted here in full:

the craft of making buttons
that we may come apart
in style

horn, pewter, even plastic

pray, sir
undo this button

oh, we would clothe the mind
in politeness, even
in extremity

to button up is seemly, to
unbutton, step
seemingly without art into
nothing, is grace

While Jones begins with 'the craft of making buttons', it's primarily ageing that concerns him, and the extended metaphor of 'unbuttoning'. The speakers in his earlier poems were often just spectators, but here the action is internal, with the poet aspiring to grace by casting off the material world. The poem itself is as stripped of artifice as the argument it presents—notice the lack of punctuation, and the way lines flow freely into one another with stanza breaks acting as long pauses. While 'Praise' is a short lyric, its loose-limbed syntax is characteristic of the lengthier poems Jones began to write as he moved closer to retirement. The best of these, 'Balthazar', 'Christmas/Going On', and 'Saint Martin/Sint Maarten' are too long to be compiled here, but are foundational for readers who want a more complete picture of Jones as a poet.

The Essential D. G. Jones is the first volume of selected poetry to span the poet's entire career. It updates his last selected, A Throw of Particles (1983), and trims the fat to present his most important lyrics. It also includes the never-before-published 'The Docks Have Been Hauled Out' and 'Suddenly', written in the intervening years since Jones's collected poems, The Stream Exposed with All its Stones (2009). Though Jones has published sparsely in the 21st century, primarily in little magazines, his output embraces the digital world's encroaching chaos, replacing each welcome face with 'a nameless music, unrehearsed'. Ultimately, his legacy is one of resolve, having shaped Canada's multicultural landscape and adopted a unique voice that looms large within the Canadian canon.

---

1. Frye, Northrop. 'Conclusion.' *Literary History of Canada: Canadian Literature in English.* Ed. Carl F. Klinck. Toronto: University of Toronto Press, 1965. 821–849.
2. Bowering, George. 'Coming Home to the World.' *Canadian Literature* 65 (1975): 7–27.
3. Jones, D. G. Untitled editorial. *ellipse* 1 (1969): 5.
4. Jones, D. G. Untitled editorial. *ellipse* 1 (1969): 5.

Portrait of Anne Hébert

The sunlight, here and there,
Touches a table

And a draught at the window
Announces your presence,

You take your place in the room
Without fuss,

Your delicate bones,
Your frock,
Have the grace of disinterested passion.

Words are arrayed
Like surgical instruments
Neatly in trays.

Deftly, you make an incision
Probing
The obscure disease.

Your sensibility
Has the sure fingers of the blind:

Each decision
Cuts like a scalpel
Through tangled emotion.

You define
The morbid tissue, laying it bare

Like a tatter of lace
Dark
On the paper.

Northern Water Thrush

The bird walks by the shore
    untouched by the falling sun
        which crashes in the alders.

Lilting on delicate feet
    among the dry reeds, the washed
        and broken skeletons of trees,

he moves through his broken world
    as one, alone surviving, moves
        through the rubble of a recent war:

a world of silence but for the sound
    of water tapping on the stones,
        a drag of wind in the pine.

Grey with his yellow, fluted breast
    he dips and halts, a string of notes
        limned on the stillness of a void:

the stillness of the early spring
    when new suns prepare
        like new buds in the leafless air

a pristine world, the old
    calligraphy of living things
        having been destroyed.

But though he walks magnificent
    upon the littered shore, holding
        the moment with his poise,

he too will whiten with the days,
    and the flawed human world
        return with his delicate bone.

Winterkill

When without warning
      winter falls upon the self,
      a piece of dung,
             white in whiter snow,
      burns within the mind more like the sun
             and is more real
      than any glittering abstract we may know.

Then must some thaw,
      some impulse in the nerve-bound heart
      release the tender shoots of sense and send
             each tendril of the brain
             into the air,
      wherein at last each thought
             may with the days
      unfold like some great flower.

Then all the world is like a girl
      whose naked presence
      haunts us in a room.

Else winter reigns throughout the self
             and we become
      more barren than the nest
      that sways within a winter wind.

Odysseus

A Monologue in the Underworld

When last did the sun
Arm with brightness all my arms, and lie
In the folds of my black sail?
Where are the bright salt waves?
And the salt flesh of the wave-born girls?

In this distance of memory they fade.
Even the image of the spoiled
City, smouldering on the morning sky,
Grows insubstantial as a shade.
Styx and Lethe, black, flow through the mind.

What cities, and men, what girls
Might have known this face, these eyes,
What faces might my eyes have known,
Since, discarding faces, lives,
I fled across the waters red with suns
In search of one face, life, and home?

About the pit of sacrifice, the fires
Like tongues thirsting for sound
Flare, and flicker on the brain.
Surrounded by the voiceless shades
Whose throats are eager for this blood, I bare
The sword of my refusal to their baleful eyes.

When will the blind man come? When
With this blood — O great communion —
May I give these shadows tongue? And sail
Outward, homeward, to a land of men?
Old shadow! from these shadows, come.

I am blind. Aiee, I am struck blind!
All those faces—all, are mine!
World upon world unfolds, salt with foam,
Or tears, with love's salt hair: cities and men,
Girls, arms and oarlocks, all the cattle of the sun.

They are gathered in the fold
Of my dark sail; they are folded in the sun.
The sun engulfs the restless sea. Not a cloud
Appears. Endless and shining, beyond all
Pillars of Hercules, lovely and tempestuous,
The ocean rolls, and rolls.

My sight returns, and darkness—
Palpable with shadows crowding to the blood;
Shadows which now speak to me of homely things
And then depart, like figures in a dream.
My men—I hear them shouting down the wind.
Oh, once again, I smell the grey, salt sea.

Beautiful Creatures Brief as These

For Jay Macpherson

Like butterflies but lately come
From long cocoons of summer
These little girls start back to school
To swarm the sidewalks, playing-fields,
And litter air with colour.

So slight they look within their clothes,
Their dresses looser than the Sulphur's wings,
It seems that even if the wind alone
Were not to break them in the lofty trees,
They could not bear the weight of *things*.

And yet they cry into the morning air
And hang from railings upside down
And laugh, as though the world were theirs
And all its buildings, trees, and stones
Were toys, were gifts of a benignant sun.

Music Comes Where No Words Are

For Peggy Atwood

Music comes where no words are
Despite the rain and gloomy days,

Like happiness without a place,
Without occasion or excuse.

And sadness colours all its notes
However pure, because, most free,

It wanders always imageless
Upon the face of possibility.

Is it love that featureless
Seeks satisfaction in a face,

Informing that which will betray
The substance of its happiness?

The world erupts into a manifold
Of features and strict melodies,

Till pretty tunes and sunny days
Are burdens of banality.

Then one welcomes gloomy days
And searches in each welcome face

Hoping to discover there
A nameless music, unrehearsed.

The Perishing Bird

The mind is not
Its own place
Except in Hell.

It must adjust, even
When the place is known.

Only time
Will tell the mind
What to think,

What birds to place
On what boughs:

The catbird crying,
'Me, me'
In a dry, hot bush,

At night the owl
Crying, 'Who?'
In a distant wood.

All else
Is an infernal shade

Where the family trees
Gather their antique
Nightingales

And the ill will
Flowers in the leaves.

For Hell's the Lord's
Bijouterie,
A Byzantine world

Where the clock-work birds
And the golden bees
Eternally repeat

What the heart once felt
The mind conceived.

For the mind in time
Is a perishing bird,
It sings and is still.

It comes and goes like the butterflies
Who visit the hill.

The cries of the children come on the wind
And are gone. The wild bees come,
And the clouds.

And the mind is not
A place at all,
But a harmony of now,

The necessary angel, slapping
Flies in its own sweat.

Cocking its head to the wind
It cries,
'Who me? Who me?'

And whatever the answer,
It forgets.

It is radiant night
Where time begets
The sun, the flowers, Nanabozho's gift —

Mosquitoes,
Who disturb my sleep —
And everything else.

Stevie and Sea

Hardly a barnacle
Stevie exults:

He is pleased with the sea,

Which round about rock
In tumble and somersault
Learns to sit up.

Crash! it recovers
Delight in disorder, lazily
Pawing the rock.

It lolls along coast.

Even the lovers lost in its thunder
Thrill to the shock.

The eye is all scenery,
Headland and heaven —

Infinite vista and the mind at play.

Eye runs to horizon, forever —
Forever gets caught,
Is taken by process: ocean

Talking with rock.

Here is no thought:
Uproar,
The stone and the splash —

Spray!

One thinks with the bone.
Stevie alone
Communicates: yellow-beaked cry.

What a ruckus! The mind
Clings like a barnacle, clings
To a thought.

Stevie
Screams with delight.

The Path

The children are running, there are four —
Five,
The children are running down the path,
Down the hill between young pine and sumac,
Between bushes,
Under the last light of the summer solstice.

One does not live here,
One is not running,
One is a girl, homesick, and older.

One is sad, her mother (running)
Is married again and lives in Toronto.

One is still hiding, stopped, behind bushes.

One is holding his foot,
He has stepped on a thorn.

One's off the horizon.

The children are running, there are five —
Four,
Down the path in the last light of evening,
Under the pink and white clouds,
Under the blue once, and forever, sky.

The Stream Exposed with All its Stones

The stream exposed with all its stones
Flung on a raw field
Is covered, once again,

With snow.

It is not hidden. It
Still flows.

The houses in the valley, standing
Motionless below,
Seem wrapped in sunlight like a snow

And are deceptive. Even stones
Deceive us.

The creator goes
Rampaging through our lives: winter
Is a masquerade.

I tell you
Nakedness is a disguise: the white
Is dark below.

This silence is the water's cry.

I tell you in those silent houses girls
Are dancing like the stones.

A Garland of Milne

He lived in the bush, the wilderness
but he made light of it

He was at home, sitting
with the small birds around him
gathering seeds, the bare

earth showing through the snow
the sun falling
scenting the air

For him it was a garden

Wildflowers picked in the woods
he placed in a pickle jar
perhaps to sketch

A tent made a pleasance

He let the trees stand where they were

and he went quietly
where islands curled up for the winter

A wife could not abide
that god-forsaken country

but a woman came
as silently as trees
and stayed

being cut in the grain, like Eve

He wanted nothing

He lay in wait for ponds, the still
moments when the snow
fell from the branches

Flowers he knew most naked in a bowl

He left it to Monet to paint
the waterlilies in their wild

and dangerous state

The titans he contained in a cartouche

A battlefield or a deserted house
had a life of its own

No violence

Who flies with the whirlwind is at rest

No one in France
could make such galaxies
of glass and water

intricate with flowers

All space came out in flowers
miraculous, erupting from a void or mouth

And every breath
a wind or sun, a season or delight
drew colour from the earth

as if a brush
stroked virgin canvas

The hills flew little flags beyond
the painting place

The darkest night drew fires
like jack-o'-lanterns from the street

The children danced like flames

And gaily, gaily glowed the islands
under the storm's spout

The light was never spent

A solemn gaiety awoke
in the white poppy

amid the sanguine and magenta reds

Spring Flowers

Apple blossom rises through
the news of war

a single branch

I am surrounded by these flowers

lily-of-the-valley in a glass
stems tangled like Ophelia's hair

and white narcissus, petals
beaded like a lover's flesh
or grass at morning

on the battlefields

These flowers
drink news out of the air

a star falls through the kitchen
and a mixed bouquet
of violets and primrose

as if war

the fighting in the desert and the smell
of oil and cordite, roar
of tanks, were but a myth

like flowers
and literature

and mounds of pale forget-me-nots

and mounds

I am surrounded by the war

That's It

That's it, walk around
in your black bra and your half-slip
half way to morning

tell me I don't understand
the weather, autumn hills, cold
mist on the water

lightning that broke through the house
and left me
sweeping up glass, all an illusion

go on shedding your clothes
like leaves of the calendar, hands
dispensing with seconds

are you trying to tell me that fall
comes before summer, bedtime's
a white dawn

I Annihilate

I annihilate the purple finch
in the apple tree

it is a winter dawn

it is 'La Guerre' Henri Rousseau
saw charging through the shattered space
of the Second Empire

it is a faint
raspberry
in the silent cosmos

c'est une tache
sur la page blanche

un cauchemar en rose

c'est le Québec
libre

a bird

c'est ça
un oiseau dans un pommier

it may fly off
but it won't go away

I neglected to mention the snow

Winter Comes Hardly

Winter comes hardly
in this part of the garden, hummingbirds
in the hibiscus, a great
cream-coloured cruise-ship sliding
in under the shadowed peaks
at dawn, a fisherman
knocking about in the moonlight
under volcanic stone, the slow
surf breaking

        the village goes on
like an eternal childhood, men
women and children, chickens and dogs
noisy and easy amid the smells
of coal-pots, copra and sulphur

market women with grapefruit
oranges and pawpaws, watercress
onions, cristophene and callaloo
early or late avocados or mangoes
bananas or breadfruit, an endless
trickle out of the hills
            fish
out of the sea
        goats, sheep, cattle
tethered at the roadside

        a constant
grinding of small cars, trucks
made buses, the wooden benches
roofs, packed with baskets, bundles
produce, a pig in a poke, all

rattling over the pocked, serpentine
mountain roads, the Star of Wonder

Do Them Back, or Kim
or Industry
                    easy
out of the sun to spend a day in the rum shop
playing cards
                    many days
felling the gommier, hewing and burning
stretching the new pirogue
Ch. Anyone, OK OK OK, or
Why Wonder, finding
cause for festivity
                    Hi, Hi
going slow, avoiding a mash-up
Hi, Hi, getting a drop, or walking
sack on the head, basket
or coal-pot or bundle of fodder

amid horns, music, the Morning
People's Show, the Creole
music from Martinique, Steel Bands, Rock
from the local Disco
                    sound
shouts, fishermen paying out net
banging the boats, banter
of market, bark
of the tipsy street-corner wit
harassing the girls with obscene
compliments, chronic laughter
wrung from the loungers
                    rain
rustling plantations, the gusts
banging the shutters
                    cocks crowing
morning or midnight, suddenly

all the dogs of the village barking
the Cinecraft rocking, 'Ee salope'
as the villain appears
in a Super-Bad Karate-Western
'Ee salope', 'Ee salope', 'Ee salope'
and on Sunday, bells
                              young girls
heads elaborately braided, wearing
petticoats, lace, their brightest
Madras, wearing white
knee-socks
                    winter is Hell
for whoever has made no confession

winter is age with her stick
moving slower than slow
is the loss of the music
                              bilharzia
and progressive anemia
                                   is the turbulent
ripple of varicose veins
over the brown skin
is a blizzard of children
                              is the seasonal
flurry of whites, the rain
of small coin
                    a small place
for Bubbles, for Sweet Drinks, for Smiley
or Martin, or Graham with his flash
enormous black and red shoes
his toque and transistor
                              for Edwin
sane now at eighty and sole
master of the white man's garden

le malheur blanc, eating away
at the body politic, another kind
of leprosy, eating away
at the stars, time, even
the white God
                    still
winter comes hardly here with bikinis
sprawled on the beaches, the body splayed
on the plastic deck, rocking
in a leeward breeze
                          like a sleek
lizard splayed in the sun high
on the patio
              winter is boredom
the slow shift of the light
filtered by shutters, the late afternoon
light under eaves, in the weathering
grain of the shingles
                          a silence
that grows with the surf, the pause
when the hummingbirds cease
to haunt the hibiscus
                        or else
the sudden bonfire flickering
high on the Piton
in the ebb of the stars, in some other
wind
      the moment when
anywhere, the mind drifts loose
from the human family
the illo tempore, the island, the broken
wall of the garden

                    when the sun
has no face, and the light is a long
irreversible snowfall
                    winter
comes subtly here
where the shell of a sea-egg lies
bleaching on the rail
                    where the glistening nude
leaves the stain of her shadow
between the sea and the sky, the peaks
and the long curving horizon

Tremor

Thunder in the earth, today
in Guatemala, the first
quivering of the floor
                              crocks
tiles falling

heaven reversed, and one goes staggering
into its silence

chicken feathers, dust
and the family effects settle
with the earth's plates

while here in Québec the snow
drifts and the pit
of an avocado splits

in a glass jar

Thunder, I ask? clearing a space
among the daily papers

One should have ears in his feet
one should read the still air
like a beast

like a seismograph
searching the silence

Even so, up, down
it is there
            in the stove
in the furnace of the stars
in the lungs
            the thunder
shaking the heart

Between Wars

Hey man, we're on the street

Like new animals infesting
your empire?

      We feed
our sex to the hunters. They
nourish our judgement

It's the neon version of Dante
right?

      You think we're dumb
We're not

      This is no
Coney Island of the Mind
This is your zoo, this is your
playpen, real as dirt

It's cold

      You see that girl
nice tits, real young
she c'n hardly talk?

You know her? No? Yeah
well don't look, man. She's
got the eyes of God

The Pioneer as Man of Letters

He took the alphabet
and dumped it in a field

Asters, buttercups, corn-
flowers formed there

Daisies winked at him
Everlasting, ferns, the wild

alfalfa made the air
articulate, glasswort

turned the gravel green
He hiccupped, hawks appeared

hepaticas, bright hips and haws
He stood amazed as inchworms

parceled out this jungle
watery acres of cattails

rocky flats of lichen
barklands of pale fungi

mushroom farms. He blinked
saw nematodes. Mosquito nymphs

swam with naiads in his mind
Such opulence, such

olfactory oddities. Muskrats
otters moved in the rivers

nudging the naked bathers
Ants milked aphids, watched

from towers of ox-eye daisies
Mites and small flies

pillaged insect orchards
The ooze stirred. At last

his erotic eye, abased
was lifted by the oriole

to tall elms, to pines
poetizing in the wind

O periwinkle, are you fish
or flower? O pis-en-lit

O Quaker ladies like the sky
He was elated. Redwings

flashing were celestial
coals, strange paracletes

announcing night. He fell
to ragweed, rhizomes, roots

recovered with Oswego tea
The smell of sweetgrass soothed him

He was saved. But then
thistles needled him, a toad

became a moving map, ticks
got under his skin. He sighed

for soapwort, saxifrage
for black-eyed Susans, found

the serpent's wisdom, soared
tipsy with swallows, sang

He was with sky, his mind
ubiquitous. His ponderations

grew like umbels on a wild
carrot. Uranus hung there

Pluto, amid vibrations
of departing light. Electrons

pions, mesons, protons
danced in a stately, large pavane

then jived up close, kept massing
branching. He saw v

and double v and ampersand
in viper's bugloss, vervain

vetch and vole and woodlouse
Wyverns rose like smoke

from the far valley. Gold warts
appeared on poplars, yeast

on a dead branch. He yelled
and finches flew, and yellow

warblers, hidden, yipped
like tiny jackals. He was x

an instrument on which they played
a kind of xylophone

riffed and rattled by
loose characters. He felt

like Ugolino in his own
spawn. He swallowed hard

thought zephyr, sifr, zilch
The sunset came in packets

fasces, whirls of yarrow stalks
But the diviner slept. Whelmed

and overwhelmed, the voice
in the whirlwind murmured zzzzz

Fatigue at Night

No more news, unless
the wind turning the leaves
No more of the things
people do, events, events
unless the wind
rolling the garden. No more
theories of life, of
particles, unless the leaves
turning the odors
of flowers, spaces
between far hills, stars
No more summits
stellar, criminal, moral
No more flowers, unless
unless, without reading
it's the wind turning the leaves
darkly, like some
irreverent whale, leviathan
loose in the garden

A Thousand Hooded Eyes

i)

The universe is a largely
dry subject, but water, o thalassa,
that is a matter

of imagination, its trickles, runnels, vast
littorals suspend
almost a page of elements

a soup, a salty sea
of discourse, it can generate
strings of sunlight, diatoms, flatworms

those wavering
soft lightbulbs (Medusa, Noctiluca) &
the glass catfish

ii)

which came first, the stomach
or the appetite to process
watery bits

o bricoler, o bricolage
let's cover the bag with scales, let's
hang it on a line

detecting tremors
let's make our own
waves, add fins

finesse, add bite
add sinister, voilà, the pike, the clown
the surgeon fish

iii)

a bad day for Beelzebub, his
minioned flies
                out of
pond matter
the belly aspires
spawns legs, the spatulate
fingers, smiles

and slippery (I love
the frogs in your jacket) dines
and climbs

replacing bee's buzz
click and drone, with the piccolo & the heavenly
trombone

iv)

the Pentagon is the simple
beginning of the turtle, the amateur
of armoured plate

provide, provide
by pushing everything aside
for the retractable

fat legs, and beak — and double it
above, below
miz and mister five by five

add packaging, the eggs transporting
sea water, the beachhead
with a thousand hooded eyes

v)

the crowned
salamander of the French
kings hides

in pockets with keys (these rings
for sale
at Chenonceau

maintained
by a manufacturer of fine
chocolates) O

sweet lizard, lockets of queens
could not contain your royal
meanderings

vi)

certain African vipers are
a macramé angels
dream of, intricate

as the forest floor, where the pretty lumps
lie like angels
still, until the busy prey

passes, passing
into their design — few
are chosen, worse

few of those elect
become truly divine
in a lady's purse (or pumps)

vii)

the alligator's motherly
and builds a nest
of brush and stuff

she cracks small turtles with
unseemly zest

she stars in films where scientist
is evil genius — who
is breakfast in the end? (you guess)

she blends
kindness with her mortal ends: swallowing
she rests, that prey

may say their orisons

viii)

   j'appelle au loin
      — Paul Piché, 25/6/90

where the twisted pines
split, in the inks of
Wei Yen, the pale bones

of tigers and dragons
— according to Tu Fu, there being
no other evidence

tonight
in Québec, the dragon is white
and blue, the

evidence ten thousand
flags in the wind, the supple
spine of song

ix)

lives in old books or
manuscripts, in
the orient

in the Chinatown
of Amsterdam, ka-bam!
outdoes

for a day
the prostitutes — a stately
clown — when other

fish, flesh, & fowl
are gone, he will swallow the stars
and lie down

Singing up the New Century

i)

the wood above, backlit in the neighbour's
floodlight, becomes a cold
music for strings

births too many and deaths violent, the world's
climate is change, it sings
little götterdämmerungs — shutting down quarrels
with flood water, bone chill, total
whiteout
        a shiver
runs through the workforce, the gross
national debt, the broker who clings
to old securities

who said the pathetic fallacy was
an invention of poets: here
the retailers can tell you that thirty days
of snow and cloud reflect
the mood of the buyers — global warming
means local cooling, a general
atmospheric depression

it's a question of finding the music, the sheer abnegation
of one or two strings
                    or slashing
black and white keys

ii)

surfing the net is no relief for the child
— though the kid carried daily
through sniper's alley in Sarajevo
smiles
      the amazing pace
of communications deludes us, like the belief
in angels — these are the wiles
of traders, swapping a few thousand baud
for our worthless skins

certain African porters told white men
a halt was imperative, however near the appointed end
since their souls
needed time to catch up — like the old
hatreds
      information
may not register in the sole or really change
the arch of the foot — walking
takes time

surfing the net is a breeze
for the child who can run — knowing
one hopes, how many lag
footsore and far from the sea, only bold
in their grief, and their dying

iii)

tonight the woods are neither dark
nor deep — how do the birds
sleep in this glare

farther out there is no power, roads closed
lines down — at least
in the Shetlands, the climate propitious
for old song
                sing
back and sides go bare, or
if a body meet a body — in Moscow even vodka
won't keep you to dawn

archaic measures

ships caught in ice, the latest ruins
frozen, and TV
the new castle, its outlying keeps in the cool
parklands of space, the hour
late, hoods on the street
or in office, it's a race, let's say a progress
towards one fatality
or another
                still
tonight in these woods there are birds
pondering song

Stumblesong

sweet stuff, a warm body
in a cold bed, a dry
endearment coming in
from the wet snow

retirement a walk
in an April
blizzard, a childhood
of aches & pains

the short time to discover
nothing is gained
certainly — going for broke
the exception

which at least
can be shared, careering
into disaster with
love or distinction

not isolate with
surgical violence or garbage
on a street, just gently
coming apart

The Cut Back Beds

delight in the amputation
of plants, stumps
of flowers, make this season
bearable

there are forms of truth

show me your scars, the
disposition of your roots, the
base plot mapped
by moles, indexed above ground
by these pale fans, these
brown straws, these limp
members

in rain or in the odd
balmy light of October — their beauty
has no ratings

there are forms of truth

the virulent
stubble of gardens, exposed
to the elements, raw
evidence of the surgeon's
ruthless desire

Epistolary

the postal code tells you nothing
about the weather
                the lights going on
in the villages, the habits
of a certain hour

                the wind
almost balmy, eating the snow

one looks at the glasses, a plate
on a counter, the mere air
given coordinates

no one else there

these arrangements are telling if
also inscrutable
                the shadow
defined by its object

the wind is delivering the mail

Grounding Sight

the star detected through the leaves
though lamplit is
a different star

the sniper in his tree
might say the same of Vega
of his targets, of
well, birds — themselves surprised
by some changed logic
puts him there

these intimacies may well define
death or distance in
distinctive ways
                    the casualty
that makes us stop the car

Praise

the craft of making buttons
that we may come apart
in style

horn, pewter, even plastic

pray, sir
undo this button

oh, we would clothe the mind
in politeness, even
in extremity

to button up is seemly, to
unbutton, step
seemingly without art into
nothing, is grace

Ideas of the End of the World

the latest: a universe
losing its gravity

it will become its own
emanation
              very thin, very cold, very dark
an enormous
unseeable haze

the forlorn bit of a juniper
stuck in a vase
looks almost abundant
                        though tonight
I can see how it bends in a wind
I can't feel

a weak vehicle, yes, its tenor
vastation

Goldfinchen

greedy guts, again and again, stack
the feeder
        distracting
from
the snow-rain-snow end
of May with
        their flashy
counterfeit
        sunshine

some of it
mint fresh

        silly coin — the cardinal
interrupts them like
  a sin

The Docks Have Been Hauled Out

when it stops raining, ducks draw
on the lake, like
sketching with quicksilver

the far shore brushed out, the park
empty of cyclists, their
spidery machines, the summer bodies
yearning towards the sun — trees
do the littering

a gull remains
inspecting the breakwater

the village retires

the line of the muskrat dissolves

this is the season the artist
unhappy, tears up
throws out, takes apart
his canvas
his brass bands, his towering
installation

he turns on the fog machine

relief

silence and void, silence and void

in a minute he'll reinvent ducks, their muttering
their quack, their invention of lines

Suddenly

a flock, a body, the birds
moving, moving the air, moving
the bank behind the house, the snow
sieved by sun and rain, the
seeds, the fallout from trees, hedge
a feeder

       nervous, a percentage of feathers
lift off, sheer off, a percentage
arrive, others remain, picking their
way, a jittery wave of scavengers, cleaners
over the snow

the body of spring engages
the body of winter engages
the body of spring, engages
feathers and debris

About D.G. Jones

D.G. (Douglas Gordon) Jones was born on January 1, 1929, in
Bancroft, Ontario. The son of Arlene Ford and Gordon Jones, his
formative years were spent on the Canadian Shield where his father
ran a lumber and pulpwood business. As a teenager Jones attended
Grove Preparatory College, before moving to Montreal and
registering at McGill University, where he pursued a degree in
English Literature. There he met Louis Dudek, who taught a part-
time night course and sparked his interest in modern American
poetry, particularly the work of Ezra Pound. With Dudek's support,
Jones published his first poems in *CIV/n* and *Contact* (a literary
magazine founded by Raymond Souster), and convened with several
of Canada's leading writers, including Irving Layton, F.R. Scott and
A.J.M. Smith.

Jones married Betty Jane Kimbark in 1950, with whom he would
have four children. Graduating from McGill with a B.A. in 1952, he
proceeded to enroll as a graduate student at Queen's University
under the direction of George Whalley, and his thesis involved
The Cantos, as well as Ezra Pound's translation of Homer's *Odyssey*,
which he'd later use to pen a short homage of his own. Earning his
M.A. in 1954, Jones subsequently accepted teaching posts at the
Royal Military College in Kingston (1954–55) and the Ontario
Agricultural College in Guelph (1955–61). It was during this time
that he published his first book, *Frost on the Sun* (1957), with Contact
Editions. Many of the poems from this collection were reprinted in
1961's *The Sun is Axeman*, a book 'dominated by summer and by
celebrations of the fullness and self-sufficiency of nature', according
to Margaret Atwood.

Moving to Québec's Eastern Townships in 1961, Jones accepted a
teaching position at Bishop's University in Lennoxville, and began
translating French-Canadian poets (many of whom he met at the
'Rencontre des poètes' retreat in 1958). Following his appointment to
the Université de Sherbrooke in 1963, where he was tasked with
building a master's program in Québécois comparative literature,
Jones would not move again. His next book of poems was *Phrases
from Orpheus* (1967), and in 1969 he founded the bilingual literary
journal *ellipse* with his second wife, Sheila Fischman. Jones's position

at a francophone institution convinced him of the importance of reciprocal translation, and he co-founded the journal *ellipse* focused on one-on-one dialogues between poet-translators.

In 1970, Jones published one of the seminal books of literary criticism in Canadian letters, *Butterfly on Rock*. With a title borrowed from Irving Layton, it would become a touchstone for students and teachers alike, and Jones urged Canadians that 'It is apparent that we must move into our own cultural house, for we are no longer at home in the houses of others.' In his personal life, he married Monique Baril in 1976, his third, and final, wife. That same year Jones was awarded the President's Medal from the University of Western Ontario for *The Lampman Poems*, and also published a book-length translation of Paul-Marie Lapointe's *The Terror of the Snows* (1976) with the University of Pittsburgh Press. The influence of Québécois poetry is evident in Jones's own work from this time, and arguably his best collection of poetry, *Under the Thunder the Flowers Light Up the Earth*, received the Governor General's Award for Poetry in 1978.

Jones received an honorary doctorate from the University of Guelph in 1983. He continued to write poetry and translate throughout the 1980s and 1990s, and he won the A.M. Klein Prize for Poetry for both *Balthazar and Other Poems* (1988) and *The Floating Garden* (1995), and a second Governor General's Award for his translation of Normand de Bellefeuille's *Categorics: 1, 2 & 3* (1992). In addition to poetry, Jones published essays on topics such as the ethics of translation, and on the work of writers like Earle Birney, E. D. Blodgett, and F. R. Scott, as he neared retirement. A lengthy article entitled 'The Hexagone Poets and the Continuing Revolution in Quebec Poetry' appeared in *Studies on Canadian Literature: Introductory and Critical Essays* in 1990.

Retiring from the Université de Sherbrooke in 1994, Jones remained active and published his final full-length collections of poetry, *Wild Asterisks in Cloud* (1997) and *Grounding Sight* (1999). He was appointed an Officer of the Order of Canada in 2007, and his collected poems, *The Stream Exposed with All its Stones*, appeared in 2009. D.G. Jones died on 6 March, 2016.

D.G. Jones: A Bibliography

POETRY

Frost on the Sun (1957)
The Sun is Axeman (1961)
Phrases from Orpheus (1967)
Under the Thunder the Flowers Light Up the Earth (1977)
A Throw of Particles (1983)
Balthazar and Other Poems (1988)
The Floating Garden (1995)
Wild Asterisks in Cloud (1997)
Grounding Sight (1999)
The Stream Exposed with All its Stones (2009)

CHAPBOOKS

A Thousand Hooded Eyes (1990)
Standard Pose (2002)

CRITICISM

Butterfly on Rock (1970)

TRANSLATIONS

Paul-Marie Lapointe. *The Terror of the Snows* (1976)
Gaston Miron. *Embers and Earth* (1984)
Paul-Marie Lapointe. *The 5th Season* (1985)
Normand de Bellefeuille. *Categorics: 1, 2 & 3* (1992)
Émile Martel. *For Orchestra and Solo Poet* (1996)